T0380708

A YOGI MAMA'S GUIDE TO YOGA, AYURVEDA & YOUR CHILD

A Book for Parents and Kids

Written and Illustrated by

Jennifer Hardy-Berthiaume

Balboa Press books may be ordered through booksellers or by contacting:

Balboa Press
A Division of Hay House
1663 Liberty Drive
Bloomington, IN 47403
www.balboapress.com
1 (877) 407-4847

Because of the dynamic nature of the Internet, any web addresses or links contained in this book may have changed since publication and may no longer be valid. The views expressed in this work are solely those of the author and do not necessarily reflect the views of the publisher, and the publisher hereby disclaims any responsibility for them.

ISBN: 978-1-9822-0386-3 (sc)
ISBN: 978-1-9822-0385-6 (e)

All hand-drawn cartoon images are by Jennifer Hardy-Berthiaume

Balboa Press rev. date: 05/17/2018

BALBOA
PRESS
A DIVISION OF HAY HOUSE

For Arlo and Amélee, my greatest teachers, and to their father, Michel, who has supported me in every "away with the wind" idea I've ever had.

Acknowledgements

Thank you Caitlin Dor, Jocelyn Segal-Townsend, Julia Lozano, Marie-Fatima Rudolf, Michael Bridge-Dickson, Nate Hendley, Sylvia Otvos, Demetra Zoubris and her amazing copy shop, Résonance Café, where I spent countless hours writing and drawing, and to the many people who read various drafts of this book. Thank you so much to Adam Thomlison and Vanessa Muri who went above and beyond with their eagle-eyes. Thank you to some of my dearest Yoga teachers who have become friends; Barrie Risman, Carina Raisman, Jayme Hernandez, Mélanie Faucher Shanti, Sonia Beaudoin and Melanie Richards. This book came together more quickly than any of us could have dreamed, and it would have been impossible without the generous hearts of many friends and teachers.

Edited by Vanessa Muri

Contents

Foreword

As a child I needlessly suffered constipation, migraines and later allergies. Yet, I was raised in a super loving athletic family. If my mom or dad had only taken the time to research a bit about how bodies work. If I had only been deeply hydrated… If my folks had only taken the time to learn about constitutions.

I grew up through the 1970s and '80s. Holistic awareness was not part of typical suburban life. Pills were the treatment for all my maladies. Doctors didn't give explanations to the root cause and simple habit changes that would have cured me.

If my mom had picked up a book like the very one you hold in your hands—*A Yogi Mama's Guide to Yoga, Ayurveda & Your Child*—I wouldn't have tried to keep myself from crying for fear the two-day headache would get worse.

My recommendation to you, dear reader: Get deeply interested in your child's constitution. Your child is already interested in who they are. Partner with them for the journey of having a body, caring for their body, learning the basics of self-care and connecting them to be the maker of simple remedies as they grow up in their bodies.

My promise to you, dear reader, is that you too will be smitten by your exploration into Ayurveda. You will learn about you, your constitution and your health history. You will take self-care and healing into your own hands. Ayurveda cured me of my constipation, migraines and allergies. Ayurveda made me into my own healer, my family healer, and a global community leader. Taking time to dig deep into Ayurveda will empower you, your family and your lives together.

Cate Stillman
Author of Body Thrive

Introduction

YOGA, AYURVEDA AND YOUR CHILD

You've picked up this book because something spoke to you. Maybe your child has been doing yoga at school or daycare and he seems to really like it. Maybe you've been doing yoga for years and are wondering how you can make it a part of your family's life. Or maybe you'd heard the word *Ayurveda* and you feel like now might be the time to discover what it's all about.

In this book we will talk about what the Western world knows as "yoga," and turn the focus to its 5,000-year-old sister-science, Ayurveda, translated as the "Knowledge of Life." You will learn about your child's *prakriti* (Ayurvedic constitution) often referred to in this book simply as their *dosha*, and how to simply incorporate easy and practical changes into your daily life to take your family's health and happiness into your hands.

I no longer find it possible to separate yoga and Ayurveda, and in writing this book, I didn't see the point of trying to. What we, in the West, call yoga (a series of *asanas* or postures—shapes we make with our bodies) is but one piece of the healing puzzle. If we want yoga to truly be healing, I believe we need to follow it in the natural direction of Ayurveda. When you've read this book, you will not be a master of this topic. (I wrote it and I'm certainly not a master.) You will, however, be armed with enough knowledge and tools to start to make very real, positive changes in your life.

The more we learn about our child's constitution (and our own, for that matter) the more we know how to be the best possible parent for our child. We understand their quirks are not flaws, and that their challenges can also be gifts. When we understand how Ayurveda applies to our child, we know how to best support and guide her as an individual, on all levels. We bring into balance body, mind and spirit.

For those of us with more than one kid, or who work with children, isn't it amazing to see how incredibly different they can be from each other? Before having my own children, I never believed how striking the dissemblance could be.

Now I have two children and can confirm that their differences are dizzying. They're two years apart and have the same parents who raised them very similarly. Aside from a few physical resemblances, however, they are nearly opposites. They act and react differently in most situations, have different tastes, preferences and behaviours. These differences can be explained through Ayurveda.

Aside from watching things play out in my family life, as a yoga teacher I started to observe the babies in my postnatal (mom and baby) yoga classes. And I observed—and still do—some of the moms in the classes, as they quite naturally look around the room and start to compare and contrast their baby to the babies beside them. Sometimes they also start to judge or worry about their very normal children. How can two babies born on the same day seem miles apart in their development?

He's nearly crawling, but my baby hardly seems interested in rolling...

Every time I look at the eczema on my child's cheeks I feel like a bad mom...

My baby hardly seems to be gaining weight, and look at that kid's rolly thighs...

My baby is the gassiest baby that ever lived!

Again, Ayurveda explains all of these scenarios and more. Every baby, child, human is beautiful and unique and perfect when we are in our *own* balance.

At first glance, this subject might seem heavy. If, as you read on, you become overwhelmed at the richness of the subject matter, please take a pause. As you begin to explore the system, it makes a lot of sense and becomes intuitive.

Please also remember that we don't need to be religious about incorporating these "rules" into our lives. If "doing Ayurveda" *perfectly* feels stressful, please don't let it. It is not easy or even practical in our society or as parents, to follow all of these guidelines to the T. If not doing it perfectly means you won't do it at all, please reconsider. This doesn't have to be black and white, you truly can just do your best.

Yoga and Ayurveda are in many ways simple and intuitive, but also complex and layered in ways I am still discovering. This book is meant to serve as an introduction to those interested, and a guide to help you bring some of these ideas into your family life.

Let yourself be gently guided. Better health and greater happiness are just a few pages away.

Keep your child's light shining with yoga

More and more parents are doing yoga with their kids or sending them to classes. Many schools and daycares are exposing children to the practice at a very young age.

When I first started teaching yoga, I taught children full-time. It was exhausting but so rewarding. A child's yoga class generally doesn't look like an adult one—we usually focus on fun and play, and pepper in some of yoga's important messages, like love, compassion and cooperation. We *moo* like cows and *meow* like cats. We don't emphasize any kind of perfection in the poses. As long as they're safe, I encourage children to be creative and curious (as I do with adult students). We explore breath, movement, sound. Does it look more like yoga or a silly interpretive dance? Maybe both!

I don't think there are many activities more important for a child to be doing.

BENEFITS OF YOGA FOR KIDS

- **Yoga gets their bodies moving**
- **It gets their hearts pumping**
- **Group classes reinforce positive interaction and cooperation with peers**
- **Yoga helps them with concentration and self-confidence**
- **Kids learn they have more strengths than weaknesses and they learn to work on their challenges in a positive way**

All of this and the ever-important "F" word: flexibility.

Not being "flexible enough" is an excuse many adults use for never making it to that first yoga class. To these adults, I say, flexibility is not important. Not the most important thing, anyway. As Judith Hanson Lasater, celebrated yoga teacher and author writes,

"Yoga is not about touching your toes, it's about what you learn on the way down."

But our kids, our five- and six-year-old kids are in yoga classes saying, "Ooh, it hurts, I'm not flexible enough…" They are too young to feel this way. Too soon, they are losing flexibility in their bodies and in their minds. They are limiting themselves before they're even in the first grade.

A few years earlier, they were quite literally sucking on their toes. *Ananda Balasana* (Happy Baby pose) gets its name with good reason. A few years earlier, *Adho Mukha Svanasana* (Downward Facing Dog pose) and *Bhujangasana* (Cobra pose) were a daily occurrence—even before they could walk.

We are born yogis. Born flexible, in every way. In a short time, we can quickly become rigid. Rigid in body, rigid in mind, rigid in spirit. Doing yoga as a child helps that *not* happen. When we keep a kid flexible, we are helping her become her best self. We are instilling confidence and helping her learn to follow her *dharma* (inner guidance).

I believe it is our duty as parents to keep our child's shining light alive, as she grows and enters a society that mostly wants her to… blend in. If we do not extinguish our child's light, but learn who she truly is, we can accompany her on her path, her dharma, every step of the way.

Saying to a child, "*Namaste,*" we are greeting her, yes, but it is an acknowledgement of the divine light within us that is recognizing the same in her. That unique light really is divine. Please, dear parent, help keep the flame ignited.

Ayurveda and optimal health

We all know a child (and maybe have one) who seems to have a perpetual runny nose or cough. We might also know kids who seem to be on one course of antibiotics after another.

Instead of treating a cold when your kid is sick, what if you could prevent the cold in the first place? Ayurveda helps us learn early warning signs and can often nip a cold in the bud. This is not the study of disease—it is the study of life. It is preventative medicine, used to treat the individual, not the symptom, even if the medicine doesn't always come in the form of pills or syrups.

As somewhat of a hypochondriac, and someone who has dealt with anxiety her whole life, having my children get sick used to send me into a panic. Full-on panic attacks. I went on anti-anxiety medication shortly after the birth of my son because I just couldn't get it together. The reality is I was nursing two kids, changing and washing double loads of diapers and barely sleeping. I didn't feel supported and I had no idea how to take care of myself. Like many other new moms in our society, I crashed and burned, largely from lack of a village.

At the time, however, I didn't clue in to any of this. One minute my daughter had a very normal heat rash and the next I was at the doctor's asking for medication because I was vomiting from anxiety and was filled with rage. Punching holes in the walls kind of rage. Understanding my Ayurvedic constitution now, the whole story makes perfect sense. At the time, I just didn't know.

Honestly, I still find it difficult when my kids get sick. But it's different now—most things are different now that yoga and Ayurveda are my… life. I generally take much better care of myself, which allows me to handle the difficult situations that come up with my kids. I have tools to use to prevent or lessen many of the illnesses that would creep into our lives. And when the kids *do* get sick, inevitably they do, I no longer feel powerless. It was the helplessness that made me anxious to the point of seeking out psychotropic drugs. It was finding the new career path, from journalist to yoga teacher, that gave me new purpose and resulted in my quite quickly self-weaning off the same medication.

Continuing on my yoga teaching path, my yoga therapy teacher Carina Raisman, said to me, "The definition of anxiety is choking, which can be interpreted as feeling stuck," and it reframed how I thought about my anxiety and the anxiety of my students and clients—forevermore. She gave the example of being in a really small room. So small you can hardly breathe. You feel as though you are choking because you're stuck inside, walls caving in. But then, out of the corner of your eye, you see a little window. And you spot another. And your heart rate slows. You see a door. You have options and solutions to get out, and you can breathe again.

Everything in life is like this. When you don't know the way out (or you don't feel like there is one) and you don't have any solutions then of course you're going to feel panicked and things will spin out of control. They can spiral fast. But yoga, meditation and Ayurveda give us all a way out. We are co-creators in our own lives.

AYURVEDA: SOME BASICS

Ayurveda teaches us that the five elements: ether (space), air, fire, water and earth make up the doshas: *Pitta* (fire, water); *Vata* (air, ether); and *Kapha* (earth, water); and that each of us is a combination of the doshas with percentages varying from person to person. The doshas and their balance at the time of your creation, the way that they combine, is your *prakriti*.

Ayurveda's goal is to keep us aligned with our own true nature.

We all have each of the elements within us, but one dosha usually predominates with another coming in closely behind to make up our prakriti; in this case, we're known as dual-doshic. Sometimes we meet people who are tri-doshic, that is to say they have an approximately equal amount of each dosha, but that's quite rare. Learning about Ayurveda is an opportunity to begin to bring the elements into balance in the most ideal way for our own personal constitution.

This ancient science teaches us how to bring a person into equilibrium—using diet, daily routine, choosing an appropriate job, activities, what climate is best to live in, and more. Ayurveda also tells us which *asanas* (yoga postures) and *pranayama* (breathing techniques) are best for our particular constitution.

Ayurveda in the Western world does not need to replace our medical system. It is complementary, although sometimes it does seem to partially replace our need for doctors because Ayurveda is preventative medicine. Like yoga therapy, we are looking at the whole person in her whole body in her whole life. A body-mind imbalanced *(vikruti)* gives way to illness, but a balanced prakriti helps prevent dis-ease. When you wrap your mind around the doshas and their qualities, you can start to see what the imbalances are and how you can help correct them to once again find homeostasis. When you learn what to pay attention to (and how) you'll start to notice your own patterns and recurring symptoms, as well as those of your child. Supporting your child's immune system by respecting his metabolic constitution is the key to health.

"Illnesses hover constantly above us, their seeds blown by the wind, but they do not set in the terrain unless the terrain is ready to receive them." — Claude Bernard

I started learning about Ayurveda first in myself. I urge any parent wanting to use Ayurveda in his or her family to do the same. I am someone who has always been known to have a bad temper. When I started to learn about my Pitta-Vata constitution, I began to realize why the "explosive personality."

How do the elements in and around our bodies work together? We know that fire is very powerful—it is essential to life. It warms us, it cooks our food, it allows us to see (thanks to the sun) and propels us forward. But out of balance, fire can be destructive and has the power to kill. How does air interact with fire?

Here's a situation I lived a few years ago as I was just starting to understand what Ayurveda is about. It was the dead of summer. I was drinking red wine and ate a couple of hamburgers, which I had doused in my favourite condiment, Sriracha (which I now know I probably don't need to be consuming). Over dinner, a small misunderstanding with a friend quickly escalated into a full-blown fight, one that lasted many months. Do I think it's because of what I was eating and drinking? Absolutely. There are of course other factors including my state of mind at that moment, and how hot it was outside that afternoon, but diet greatly impacts our emotions. For better or worse. All this, combined with the fire burning inside me, it was just way too much heat. Kaboom. This unfortunately is not an isolated incident. Any fiery parents out there might feel this is uncomfortably familiar.

I quickly realized how incorporating Ayurveda into my life could help me at least minimize situations like the one above. I began to study with various teachers in Montreal, including Dominic Tambuzzo and Annik Baillargeon.

I allowed Ayurveda to infiltrate my life in a way that was so much more than theoretical. I drank it up—I embodied it. Or it embodied me. On our family vacation to the beach, I took it all in: I felt the rough texture of the sand, the coolness of the wind and heat of the sun on my skin all at once. I watched the tide come in, wind pushing waves, waves moistening the sand and turning it to mud. I watched the heat of the sun evaporate the water, leaving the sand once again hot and dry.

I studied daily and went on to become an Ayurvedic Lifestyle Consultant with Dr. David Frawley at the American Institute of Vedic Studies. Every day of my life I still learn more from books, my teachers, children, students, strangers and the natural environment. Like yoga, there is no end to learning this subject. Even just scratching the surface of this ancient wisdom can be life-changing.

I'm not saying yoga and Ayurveda have completely removed any trace of this fire (Pitta) from my life. Thankfully, because if it did, maybe I wouldn't have had the drive to put this book out. But it has significantly helped me keep my temper under control. In the same way, my understanding of Ayurveda has calmed but not extinguished my anxiety (a Vata tendency). We're not trying to erase these (sometimes less-desirable) parts of ourselves or our children. Pitta is only a "problem" when it's lacking or in excess: out of balance and out of control.

Knowing this has, above all, changed and improved the way I parent my two children.

You see, I gave birth to my mini-me. Not only does this child look just like me, but we have a similar constitution. While she reflects back to me many of the things I may not want to recognize in myself (because we are so similar), I can also understand her better than most people will ever be able to. I can anticipate certain actions and reactions and depending on a few factors, I can often help her avoid a whole lot of pain and tears. A simple example, and one you'll see in the Flamey Jayme story on (Page 15), is that knowing my girl's tendency to get "hangry" (angry when hungry), I can make sure to have food and water handy. I always have extra for myself, too.

My son, as I mentioned, is very different from his older sister. He has a bit of fire but has a great percentage of Kapha. His metabolism is such that he can go a lot longer without eating, and happily plod along. While my girl has the tornado-like energy of the wind, which has her running, jumping and climbing anything she can find (like Frilly Millie, Page 9), he is slow and steady. He'll spend many hours focused on his drawing or Lego constructions like Matteo Potato (Page 20). The stereotype we hear about girls and boys and their energy doesn't always resonate *chez moi*. Ayurvedic constitution, however, is right on, every time. Because there's no way to measure our makeup that is more specifically personal.

I'll admit that even as a yoga teacher, I'd heard about this Ayurveda thing and thought it might be a little like opening up the newspaper and reading the very general horoscope printed for you. But again, and again I watch the truth of Ayurveda reveal itself. It allows me to be more understanding and compassionate and less judgmental. Bringing Ayurveda into my daily life as a woman and mother has been life changing, and I hope it will be the same for you.

We are who we are and we need people of all walks of life to keep things interesting. It is because of our unique constitutions that we all have special gifts to offer this world. Our goal here is to honour our constitutions and the constitutions of our children, in order to stay happy and healthy in all areas of life.

In the following pages of this book, you will meet three very different children. You will see some of your child's tendencies in one or two of these siblings. Some of the things they do, the ways they act and react, might register to you as "good/positive" or "bad/negative."

We might be resistant to recognizing some of these "negative" characteristics in ourselves, and we might covet what we see in the doshas we seem to be lacking. We might wish to be of the rare tri-doshic type (because certainly that's the best and most balanced…?) It's really not. Whatever constitution we are born with is the best constitution for us—when it's in balance.

No dosha is "good" or "bad." Yoga and Ayurveda do not work this way. What you want to label as bad, could in fact be an imbalanced aspect of the dosha, and it's these aspects that we as human beings tend to focus on. We use Ayurveda to uncover more and more of the "positive" side of our prakriti as well as more clearly beginning to see our true nature. Or that of our child.

"You're away with the wind!"

The teacher said and Frilly Millie tilted her head.

"I asked you a question, or did you not hear?

Do I have to glue your bum to that chair?"

Millie was indeed a mile away

Dreaming of all the fun games she could play

In class, she felt bored, she wanted to climb

On fences and trees—whatever she could find

Her mom calls her "Monkey,"

Her dad calls her "free,"

Her brother calls her "Millie the Buzzingbee."

11

It's true that Millie finds it hard to sit still

She'd rather be hiking mountains, or at least tall hills

Though sometimes when she's on her way somewhere

She can't remember why she was going there

And sometimes all the thinking makes Millie worry

She tosses and turns when she should be sleepy

And she gets cold quickly and needs to keep warm

With soups and stews and sweaters worn

In time Millie will learn how to direct

The beautiful power she's been gifted with

She'll learn how to balance her energy—light, floating, free

Rooting down like a solid oak tree

We need girls like Millie to grow up and invent

The coolest things we haven't dreamt up yet

FLAMEY JAYME

PITTA GIRL

Raaaaaawr!!!

From the other side of the door someone might have thought there was a tiger in the room

But it was Flamey Jayme, Pitta Girl, whose fire was letting loose

She was tired, she was hungry, she felt burning hot

It was time for a snack but Jayme forgot

"Raaaaaawr!!!" she shouted again, and her face turned bright red

Oh how she wished she felt cool instead

She rolled her tongue and breathed in like a straw

She exhaled loooong

Soon it felt like nothing was wrong

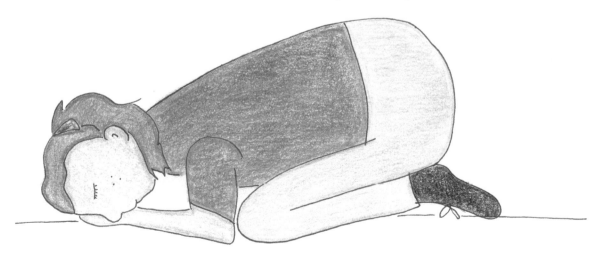

She accepted the water her mama had offered

She took a Child's pose to rest on the cool ground

Inhale… Exhale… Inhale… Exhale

She smiled and crunched a cucumber

Her favourite snack to calm all that fire

She also loves watermelon, a sweet, cooling treat

That tastes oh so good and helps mellow the heat

When Jayme takes the time to eat well and rest

That's when she's at her very best

She knows what she wants and gets things done

She has patience for work and energy for fun

"I'm sorry," she told her mama. "I know.

Now what do you say we go play in the snow?"

Matteo Potato
Kapha Boy

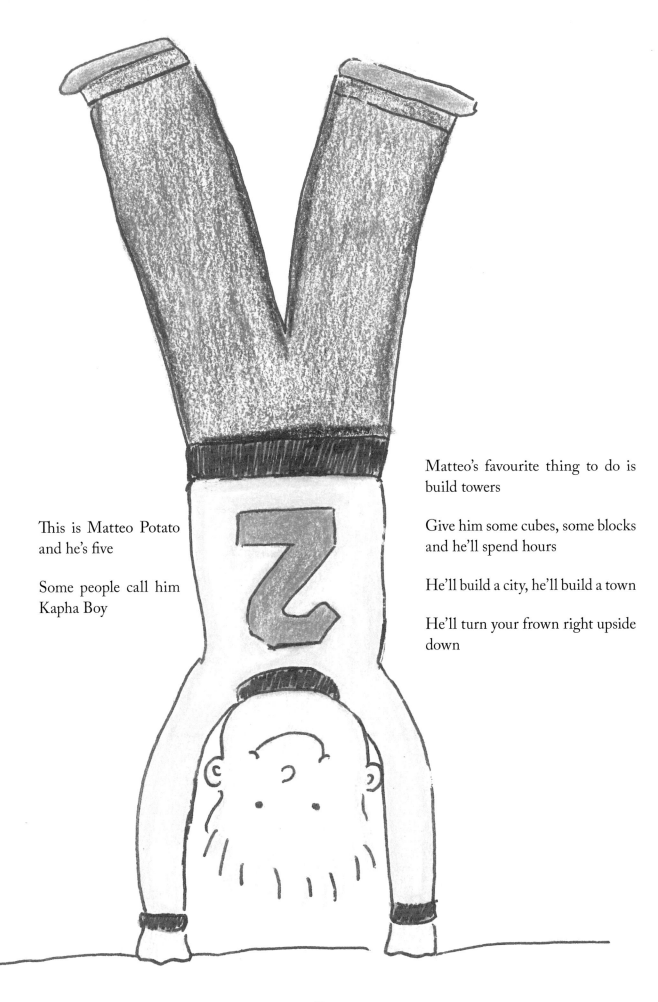

This is Matteo Potato
and he's five

Some people call him
Kapha Boy

Matteo's favourite thing to do is
build towers

Give him some cubes, some blocks
and he'll spend hours

He'll build a city, he'll build a town

He'll turn your frown right upside
down

Matteo likes to paint, draw and colour

He loves his dad and he loves his mother

He loves Sister #1 and Sister #2

If he knew you, he'd love you, too

Some people say Matteo's got a sweet tooth

And he certainly loves a big bowl of fruit

Enjoying yummy foods like spinach, squash and broccoli

Is the best thing he can do for his growing body

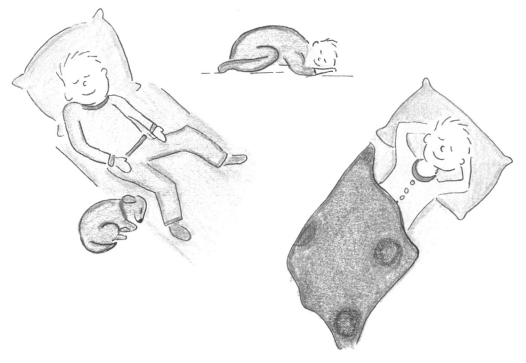

Matteo loves to sleep and could dream away

The bulk of almost every day

He'd like to watch the TV all day too

If that's what his mother would let him do

Matteo doesn't love sports or like to swim

The thought of freezing water doesn't appeal to him

He'd rather spend his time inside

With his puppy, Tony, by his side

There's no better friend a kid could find

Than Matteo Potato, of the Kapha kind

Strong as an ox and steady as a rock

Matteo Potato and his building blocks

Discover your child's unique makeup (prakriti)

It is said that we are born with our prakriti (our metabolic constitution). We inherit the dosha (elements) from our parents and myriad factors at the time of conception. In the first weeks of life the constitution starts to settle, and you'll get more clues about your child's prakriti as he or she gets a little older.

As we age, external factors knock us off balance. For example, the majority of those of us living in North America probably have way more Pitta and Vata influences and imbalances because of the go, go, go society we live in. It's important to note that you can have an imbalance, or an excess of a dosha that isn't such a big part of your own makeup. Someone who is predominantly Kapha could have an excess of Pitta, for example, and this is one way the body begins to see "dis-ease." We want to come back to that homeostasis. As mentioned earlier, it is quite rare to be an equal balance of all three, and also rare to be made up of a solo dosha.

Here is a quiz to help you get an idea of what your child's makeup is. You can use it for yourself, too. Keep in mind, it's only a guide and it doesn't replace going to see an Ayurvedic consultant, practitioner or doctor. You can circle more than one letter, if applicable. Tally up the numbers and read on for results. Usually you and your child will each be a relatively obvious combination of two constitutions. In terms of skin colour and other elements that seem specific to race, keep in mind that everything is relative. Comparing shades of skin or hair to that of your family members might be helpful.

KIDS' DOSHA QUIZ

1. **Your child's hair is:**

   A. dry, thin or curly

   B. silky, straight, blonde, red or light-coloured

   C. thick, lush, strong

2. **Your child's mouth:**

   A. lips are thin

   B. medium thickness

   C. full lips

3. **Your child's teeth are:**

   A. crooked or crowded

   B. regular and off-white

   C. large, white, straight, well-spaced

4. **Your child's skin is:**

   A. dry, rough, cool

B. pink, reddish, rosacea or freckled

C. cool, pale, oily

5. **Your child's eyes are:**

   A. dark, darting, intense, small

   B. sharp, bright

   C. big, round/blue eyes

6. **Your child's frame is:**

   A. willowy, lanky or small

   B. medium build, with good muscle tone

   C. big boned, with some extra weight

7. **Your child's circulation:**

   A. hands and feet are often cold

   B. sweats at night or during physical exertion

   C. hands get clammy

8. **More of an emotional tendency toward:**

   A. anxiety/creativity

   B. anger/determination

   C. depression/compassion

9. **When your child is upset, there is a tendency to:**

   A. cry

   B. argue

   C. turn inwards

10. **Your child's confidence:**

    A. a little shy

    B. outgoing

    C. quiet inner-confidence

11. Your child's appetite:

    A. irregular, erratic, picky

    B. a "good," regular eater

    C. enjoys eating, has a sweet tooth

12. Your child eats:

    A. quickly

    B. medium speed

    C. slowly

13. Your child's digestion:

    A. irregular bowel movements, gassy, constipated

    B. regular, soft, sometimes loose bowel movements

    C. regular, slow, thick bowel movements

14. Your child's learning and memory:

    A. learns quickly and forgets quickly too

    B. grasps things at an average rate and has a good memory

    C. learns slowly but has great long-term memory

15. Your child's strength/energy level:

    A. has lots of energy bursts, sometimes seems hyper

    B. very strong, can persevere

    C. slow and steady like a marathon runner

16. Your child prefers:

    A. warm weather to cold

    B. cool weather—forest more than the beach

    C. warmth to dampness

17. Your child's sleep:

    A. is light, disrupted

    B. is sound

    C. is blissful, heavy

18. Your child's mood is:

    A. swingin'; highs and lows can be extreme

    B. can be quick to anger

    C. generally good natured and calm

19. At play:

    A. very creative

    B. likes to lead

    C. content to play alone, focused

Mostly A's: Vata

About your Windy Kid (Vata)

It might be hard for your Vata Baby to gain weight. She tends to be gassy or constipated, have weak or variable digestion and unpredictable bowel movements. She might be called "colicky." Her sleep can be restless, she might startle easily, and she might generally be nervous. Her eating is not always predictable. She is the baby that rolled, crawled, babbled, talked and walked earlier than her friends.

Your Windy Kid has sharp features and dark, darting eyes. Her skin can be dry, her hair thin. Her body is light and delicate—long and willowy. As the child grows, you'll notice she learns easily, but forgets just as easily. Though the above stories showed Jayme forgetting to snack, forgetfulness is a quality that belongs more to her sister Millie.

She is active and creative. She might have a hard time sitting still in class and concentrating because her mind is just so busy thinking up all kinds of wonderful things. She might also be moody as a baby, child, teenager and adult—big highs and lows. Ayurveda considers disorders like ADD and ADHD Vata disturbances. Approaching these disorders from an Ayurvedic perspective, even in conjunction with Western medicine, can be incredibly helpful.

Advice from the Mama of a Windy Kid: Help her keep her feet on the ground. Actually, let her climb, because she'll probably be the kid who climbs a tree so high that all the other parents get nervous. But do help her, especially before bed, to come back down to earth. Oil massage is very helpful for this, even if it's just a little bit on the feet. (See Page 41 for more details.) Keep her warm with heavy, cozy blankets, especially in winter.

She will have a million and one amazing ideas but bringing them to fruition is the challenge. Help her follow through, as it will likely be a theme her entire life. It might be hard to stay organized at school, and she might have a messy room. Many Vata adults find themselves in the same boat with work and housekeeping.

Vata people often worry and can tend toward anxiety. Help your child find tools to calm her mind and stay in the present moment. Yoga, meditation and mantra are perfect for this (Page 45).

VATA

in balance	imbalanced
energetic, understands things quickly, creative, flexible	indecisive, hyperactive, anxious, nervous, disruptive

Mostly B's: Pitta

About your Fire Child (Pitta)

As a baby, a Fire Child might be bald for a long time! (In adults, Pitta imbalance can cause hair loss, *khalitya* and premature greying, *palitya*.) It is not uncommon to see eczema and other rashes on her skin. She will often hit developmental milestones when the textbooks say she should. She is determined, knows what she wants, and has the drive to achieve all of her goals. You will see this manifest at a very young age.

Your Pitta Kid will have blonde, brown or red hair (once it comes in). The stereotype of the "fiery redhead" exists with good reason—freckles are a sure sign there's some Pitta in there somewhere. She might be argumentative and grow to be someone who loves a good debate. She's sharp as a tack and doesn't miss a thing. Fire Folk are often very competitive. That drive can also burn her out.

Pittas are not always the easiest people to be around. In fact, they often to prefer to be by themselves. They might subscribe to the "if you want something done right, do it yourself" mentality. For this reason, they make excellent entrepreneurs. It would be difficult to run a successful business without a good amount of fire to keep you going. On the same note of being driven and successful, Pitta people, including children, can have perfectionist tendencies.

What happens when a Pitta Kid doesn't get what she wants? She's likely to get mad—and fast. She will have more tantrums than her less fiery siblings or peers—especially if she has not eaten or had enough water. Pitta people have a strong appetite and good metabolism. They are muscular, strong, and of average weight and height.

Advice from the Mama of a Fire Child: Always have food and snacks in your bag. Offer food and water *before* the meltdown. If he or she is school-aged, make sure there are extra snacks available and she knows how important it is for her mood to remember to stay hydrated. Encourage your Fire Child to rest and slow down. She might enjoy competitive team sports, but you might also have her in an activity like swimming that will literally cool her down. Being in nature is great for a Pitta child—think forest hike. Just not at noon in the blazing sunshine. I learned that one the hard way.

PITTA

in balance	imbalanced
courageous, independent, friendly, warm, leader	aggressive, angry, tantrums, controlling

Mostly C's: Kapha

About your Earth Child (Kapha)

As a new baby, he gains weight easily and eats constantly. He has big eyes (blue or light brown), long lashes and thick hair. These are the "easy babies," the "good kids." Kapha Kids are laid back, pretty calm and tend to be good sleepers.

Your Earth Child has a great vitality—a good immune system. He will generally move more slowly than the kids around him. He might speak later, crawl or walk later—think slow and steady. He has a great memory. As a toddler, a Kapha Child will have fewer tantrums and share toys easily.

Out of balance, (excess) Kapha can cause lethargy, obesity and too much mucus leading to cold and sinus issues. Digestion can be slow, bowel movements thick. Swimming isn't the best activity for him; the dampness can be aggravating. He does not necessarily have the same drive as a Pitta Child and needs some more fire in his life to get up and at 'em. As implied in the Matteo Potato story, Kapha people are generally loyal and compassionate. They become attached in healthy and unhealthy ways (depending on the balance of their makeup).

Advice from the Mama of an Earth Child: Encourage him to pursue any activity he shows an interest in, *especially* physical activities. He might be super content to sit and play Lego (or video games for that matter), so find fun reasons to get outside and get moving.

You want to find a physical activity he can excel in, enjoy and feel proud about. This will foster confidence in sport so he keeps his body moving, and hopefully this tendency will carry on into adulthood. Although Kapha people are generally hardy, a long list of diseases can be attributed to excess Kapha—they are susceptible to coughs, colds, asthma and illnesses affecting the ears, nose, throat, chest and respiratory system. Obesity is a real risk for the Kapha child and adult, as well as any diseases that can snowball from excess weight—diabetes and cardiovascular diseases—hence the importance of keeping the child moving and enjoying and valuing exercise his whole life.

Let him cry

Kaphas are peacekeepers. They don't like conflict and they don't want to rock the boat. When something is upsetting them, unlike their Pitta friend who will let you know about it, they are more likely to internalize their emotions and repress feelings, leading to many possible health issues. Remind your Kapha Kid it's okay and healthy to cry.

In Ayurveda, the suppression of natural urges, of which there are 13, is considered one of the main ways to get sick. Crying is included in this list along with urinating, passing gas and yawning... these things are meant to leave our body and it's unhealthy on many levels to stop the natural process. So, cry, baby, cry. I feel like it's especially important as the mother of a Kapha Boy to remember this, in a culture where we mostly teach that boys don't cry.

KAPHA

in balance	imbalanced
peaceful, calm, patient, devoted, loyal	lethargic, greedy, clingy, hoarding

IN CONSIDERATION OF THE SEASONS

Ayurveda is all about cycles, taking into account those of nature and time. Unlike much of Western thinking, which is very linear, Eastern thought is more circular and cyclical. How do these cycles affect us and our children?

Each of the doshas has qualities, and they become easier to see when we observe them in nature and the seasons. When considering your own dosha and your child's dosha, what to do and what to eat, it's also important to think about what season it is. This means that regardless of your child's dosha, you're going to make adjustments based on the time of year.

Late fall to early winter: Vata (ether, air) season

Tornadoes. I think of a spinning tornado when I think of Vata Children (and adults). Vata is light and cold, agitated and dry.

Vata accumulates in summer and is provoked in fall and early winter. It is alleviated in late winter. Personally, I begin to "feel Vata" every fall, and didn't understand what I was feeling until I started to better understand Ayurveda. I feel like I am going to be carried away with the wind. I become anxious and it is hard to sleep. I now know what I need in terms of diet, massage and asana to make this time of year less terrifying.

Summer: Pitta (fire, water) season

The sun is the best example of Pitta in nature. Some of Pitta's qualities are hot, light, moist and sticky.

Pitta accumulates in late winter and spring, is provoked in summer and alleviated in fall and early winter. I find summer even more difficult than the fall. I dislike the humidity in the climate I live in and I become hot very fast. So I have learned to stay out of the sun, to cut down on any foods which make the fire even stronger, and I drink teas and eat foods which are cooling.

Late winter into spring: Kapha (water, earth) season

This one is easy to feel. Kapha is slow, cold, moist, heavy and soft.

In the spring, things begin to melt and become muddy. Kapha accumulates in the fall and early winter, is provoked in late winter and spring and alleviated in summer. At this time of year, my Kapha (-Pitta) boy will throw himself on the ground kicking and screaming to NOT GO OUTSIDE. He can't stand the dampness and really looks forward to the summer.

The shift from spring to summer aggravates Pitta, from fall to winter aggravates Vata

and winter to spring aggravates Kapha.

We need to keep in mind the season we're in and the qualities of that season when we plan what to eat and feed our children.

FOOD AND AYURVEDA

Diet is obviously not the only focus of Ayurveda, but it's pretty central, and learning about food from this perspective is one of the most effective tools I found in upping my family's health game. Food is one of the most simple and effective ways we can use Ayurvedic principles to help our children. It's not about putting your child on a diet, but keeping in mind the elemental qualities in your child and in the food you are providing.

Food will have the highest value, nutritionally and energetically, when it's fresh, local and organic. Of course this is not always possible; we do our best.

The way food is prepared also affects the quality—microwaving, frozen foods (microwaving frozen foods) and canned foods are less healthy nutritionally and energetically than fresh foods.

Supper is a time that is very important for many families to connect. For some families, it's often the only time during the week that they are all together. Let this time be as peaceful as possible. (I'm a mom of two little kids, so trust me, I know this is a big ask!) But try to keep the conversation pleasant, avoiding subjects that might upset you or your little ones. Our environment and eating habits are very important for proper digestion.

"Meal time with your kids is not just about the foods and nutrients they ingest. It's about nourishment, relationship, and communication. Keep mealtimes pleasant by avoiding power struggles about who is eating how much of what. Your role as a parent is to choose the menu and set up the environment; after that, let your kids decide how much they eat."

~ Katja Leccisi, MS, RDN, Author of *How to Feed Your Kids: Four Steps to Raising Healthy Eaters.*

A few more tips:

- Eat mindfully, pay attention to your chewing
- Eat when you're hungry
- Don't eat too much
- Don't eat during screen time
- Don't eat while walking or standing

The six tastes and their heating and cooling actions (*virya*)

As you begin to incorporate simple dietary adjustments into your life, you can certainly just follow one of the many available lists of what is appropriate for your child's makeup. But the six tastes are the base from which the lists come. Each food has a taste and a quality, and you want to choose foods, usually, that are the opposite of the dosha you are trying to bring into or keep in balance.

THE SIX TASTES

sweet (earth and water)	cooling, damp, heavy, increases Kapha, decreases Vata and Pitta	i.e. fruit, sugar, milk, grains
sour (earth and fire)	heating, light, damp, increases Kapha and Pitta, decreases Vata	i.e. fermented foods, including yogurt
salty (water and fire)	heating, heavy, damp, increases Kapha and Pitta, decreases Vata	i.e. seaweed, natural salts
bitter (air and ether)	cooling, dry, light, increases Vata and decreases Pitta and Kapha	i.e. dark leafy greens, herbs, spices
astringent (earth and air)	cooling, dry, heavy, increases Vata, decreases Kapha and Pitta	i.e. raw fruits and vegetables, legumes
pungent (fire and air)	heating, light, dry, increases Vata and Pitta, decreases Kapha	i.e. garlic, herbs, spices, hot peppers

The energetic qualities and the gunas

With some practice you can *feel* the energetic quality of a food, herb or spice. If you know your Frilly Millie needs foods that ground her, you can think of the heavier stews or avocados. They *feel* heavier. What will provide some moisture for her airy body? Certainly not popcorn or kale salad. What can you serve Flamey Jayme to cool her flames or Matteo Potato to lighten him up a little? Find the opposite quality of food, herb or spice.

Weight: light and heavy

Moisture: dry and wet/damp

Temperature: cold and hot

The three *gunas* of prakriti are present in everything in varying amounts, like the beach example. In a human being they are constantly fluctuating. They are from where the doshas are born. This is a huge subject that many brilliant people have written very big books about. I'm not going to do that, but I feel that a book about Ayurveda, no matter how introductory, would be incomplete if the gunas were left out. See if you can notice how these qualities are present in the three doshas.

Sattva

Think: goodness, harmony, joy, peace, balance, light… this is what we are all kind of striving for if we are on a path to understanding Yoga and Ayurveda. We want to feel balanced and healthy in our body, mind, spirit. Understanding our constitution allows us to adjust diet, routine, etc. to work towards getting back to the mind's true nature, and to be able to see things more clearly. Sattvic food is fresh and juicy, easy to digest (could be raw or cooked). It is real, whole, clean food. It's the food you feel great after eating.

Rajas

Some of the qualities of rajas are energy, movement, change, action, distraction, passion, attachment, and turbulence. There can be an element of egoism. This is where many of us are most of the time, moving forward with careers and raising our families. It's not "bad," it's fluid and fluctuating. Stimulants increase rajas, as does too much exercise or work. Foods like garlic, caffeine and eggs are rajasic.

Tamas

Some of the qualities of tamas are darkness, dullness, inactivity and inertia. Tamas comes from ignorance, degeneration and death. It is increased by tamasic foods and routines. Meat and heavy greasy foods that might seem like a good idea at the time. Like poutine… If you're not familiar with this Quebec specialty, poutine is a pile of fries topped with a mountain of cheese curds and gravy. It usually feels pretty heavy in the gut even though it was enjoyable on the way down.

Diet and your Vata Child

A Windy Kid, like Millie, does not need food to lighten her, she needs food to ground her down—heavier foods. An avocado is heavy, beef is heavy, kale and lettuce are light and filled with air. Foods like cabbage, cauliflower and broccoli will make your Vata Child even gassier. You would not want to serve a cold, raw kale salad to your Vata Kid as we're entering the autumn and early winter months (Vata season). I would be reluctant to serve many raw veggies at all. A root vegetable soup or stew, however, is perfect, as well as warm drinks—it sounds obvious put like this, doesn't it? Encourage your Vata Child not to eat too much right before bed. Sleep can be challenging enough without digestion taking place.

Here are some favourite foods for Vata. Keep in mind that cooked foods are generally better.

Fruit

bananas	berries
melon	apples and applesauce
mango	dates and figs

Cooked root **veggies** are the best for a Windy Kid, and raw, light veggies less-so. They will be gassier, so foods like broccoli and cabbage should be minimized.

asparagus	avocado
peas	green beans
squash	sweet potato

Grains: Rice, quinoa and cooked oats are grounding and comforting. Avoid or minimize popcorn. She'll be popping all over the room!

Legumes: Vata people will support beans and pulses less than a Pitta person. Red lentils are okay, as is miso and most tofu products.

Dairy is generally balancing for Vata. Maybe not ice cream in the winter, but… cheese, ghee, fresh yogurt, warm milk (or even better, golden milk, see Page 44) and butter are all fair game.

Nuts and seeds are fantastic for Vata.

Meat: If your child eats it, heavy gamey meats are best to avoid, but she can eat red meat that a Pitta might want to minimize.

For a full list of foods to favour and avoid for Vata, see: ayogimamasguide.com/vata

Diet and your Pitta Child

A Fire Child, just like a Pitta Mama in the heat of summer (Pitta season) does not need to be eating lots of spice or heating foods like red meat or fermented foods (including yogurt).

She needs cooling foods and can get away with eating more ice cream than some of her friends. Hydration is of the utmost importance for a Pitta Child. Foods like watermelon, cucumber can even be added to water. Ayurveda, like Traditional Chinese Medicine, favours cooked food for digestion, but if there was a dosha and a season to eat raw vegan diet, it would be Pitta. Raw food is chock full of *prana* (life-force) and is used when cleansing the body. How does that change in winter? Winter is going to decrease Pitta simply because it's winter. So even though your child has high amounts of fire, it would be advisable to stay away from cold, raw, foods.

Jayme should probably not have eaten a cucumber just before heading out to play in the snow with her siblings. Who wants ice cream in the winter anyway…? In general, you would want your Fire Child to avoid acidic, spicy and sour foods.

The taste "sweet" is *cooling*. Many, but not all fruits are sweet. Here are a few examples:

apples (sweet) and apple sauce	sweet oranges
watermelon	berries and cherries
dates and figs	avocado

Good veggies for Pitta are a little sweet and either bitter, astringent, or both. Pitta kids will feel lucky to have an excuse to avoid the spicy veggies like garlic and onions.

broccoli	collard greens
asparagus	root veggies
potatoes and sweet potatoes	squashes

Choose grounding, cooling, sweet, dry grains like:

granola	oats	
pasta	quinoa	rice

Most legumes will be good for Pitta because they are astringent (cooling).

Avoid fermented soy, but enjoy black beans, chickpeas, and lentils.

Nuts and seeds can be heating and oily, but almond, coconut and flax are good.

Meat: White meats like chicken and white fish are better for Pitta than red meats.

Dairy: Ghee is great, cow and goat milk, too, as well as butter and soft cheeses.

For a full list of foods to favour and avoid for Pitta, see: <u>ayogimamasguide.com/pitta</u>

Diet and your Kapha Child

The Earth Child needs the opposite of his Windy counterpart. He is grounded, so we need to lighten him up a little—put a little pep in his step. Spices to stimulate. Maybe not a raw cayenne pepper, but many spices will be helpful for a Kapha Child; cinnamon tends to be a favourite as it's warming but also sweet. In Kapha season, most children (as children are in Kapha time of life—with Pitta in the middle of life and Vata in later life), especially Kapha Kids, should minimize dairy as, according to Ayurveda, it increases mucus and congestion. Avoid heavy, oily and sweet food.

Kapha Kids should avoid or minimize dense, heavy or watery fruits. Reach for:

mangoes	peaches
berries	pears
apples and applesauce	

Astringent, pungent and bitter veggies should be the centre of your Earth Child's diet.

asparagus	eggplant
broccoli	leaks
peas	green beans

Grains: Because they are so heavy, minimize the child's intake of oatmeal and pasta. Favour lighter grains like:

corn	quinoa
millet	buckwheat

Legumes: Most are fine for Kapha and are helpful because of their astringent quality. Avoid heavier kidney beans and miso.

Dairy should be minimized or avoided for the Earth Child. It is heavy and increases mucus. If your child has a cold coming on you would want to think about stopping dairy immediately, and definitely not right before bed. Kapha Kids are the most mucusy of kids, and especially in the winter/spring, they're going to over-produce. Just like the example of Fiery Jenny in her mid-30s (Pitta time) eating red meat with hot sauce in the middle of summer—Pitta overload! Similarly, an Earth Child (Kapha) in springtime (Kapha), eating dairy (Kapha-increasing)—it's all just too much and asking for a cold to come on. Goat milk is lighter and almond and nut milks are good.

Nuts and seeds can be too heavy. Soaked almonds are the best, and pumpkin, chia and flax are the best seeds for Kapha.

Meat is best for Kapha when it's light, like chicken, fish and shrimp.

For a full list of foods to favour and avoid for Kapha, see: ayogimamasguide.com/kapha

Tastes to balance	Tastes that aggravate
VATA: sweet, sour, salty	**VATA:** bitter, pungent, astringent
PITTA: sweet, bitter, astringent	**PITTA:** sour, salty, pungent
KAPHA: pungent, bitter, astringent	**KAPHA:** sweet, sour, salty

Vegetarianism

There is a misconception that all yoga teachers in the West are vegetarian, vegan even. It is a stereotype and nothing more. People who teach yoga classes come in all shapes and sizes and have all sorts of beliefs. I might be able to count the vegetarian, yoga teaching, white, Western friends I have on one hand. And many of my friends are white, Western yoga teachers. It's just that most of them eat meat.

Can you *really* be a "yogi" and eat meat? Not a question I'm going to answer. But there are many reasons Ayurveda favours a vegetarian diet. Firstly, a vegetarian diet is mostly sattvic. On the flipside, meat is tamasic. Its qualities can increase agitation and conflict, breed *ama* (accumulation of toxins) and feed infection.

Then there is the question of *karma*, an important concept in yoga. Karma is the Sanskrit word for "action," and as Newton says, "Every action must have a reaction." Is the reaction instant? Not necessarily, though that's how we tend to understand it in North American culture. My daughter teases her brother and then immediately trips and hurts herself—we can't help but say it's karma. It is not only actions but words and thoughts that cause "bad karma." The good news is we can also accumulate "good" karma too, to sort of balance out the rest.

Thirdly, *Ahimsa*, the first Yama of Patanjali's Yoga Sutras. It's most often translated as non-violence, although I prefer "compassion" as a translation. Factually speaking, there is a certain amount of violence inherent in the act of slaughtering an animal for its meat. There is also undeniable negative impact on the environment thanks to modern farming practices. Damage to Mother Earth is considered a form of violence.

With all of this said, Ayurveda tends toward a vegetarian diet and advises eating meat when it is life-saving and is used as a medicine.

This book wasn't written to convert you to vegetarianism, and you may not even feel it's your decision to make for your child anyway. My kids aren't vegetarian, but we are very aware of all that's wrapped up in the consummation of factory-farmed meat. Obviously, meats without antibiotics and growth hormones are way healthier, and the less pain an animal suffered, theoretically the better karmically.

NOSE, MOUTH AND EAR CARE

Nasya (Ayurvedic nasal therapy)

It is important to keep the nasal passages clean, with saline water, and lubricated with oil. Adults can use a neti pot, as can kids as they get older. It's a special little pot with a spout, filled with warm distilled or previously boiled water and non-iodized salt to make a saline solution. You use it to pass water through the nasal passages, clearing away unwanted mucus. Plastic ones are easily available at most pharmacies, health food stores and online, and they often come with prepackaged salt mixes you can add to your clean water. Ceramic ones are nice, but after having two accidentally smash I think I'm going to stick with plastic until I'm an empty nester.

At almost seven my daughter became a neti pot believer. In winter, she was sick of the congested nose that was causing her to wake up coughing at night, and I urged her to at least try the neti pot. The first time I helped her, and now she actually asks to do it, knowing what relief it will bring. At five, my son fails to understand the benefits. If they are too young to use a neti pot, there are many products now available that allow a strong enough flow of saline water to cleanse a child's nasal passages. Dropping saline water in the nose usually isn't quite enough. Please note the importance of using sterile water so you don't introduce infection.

It might seem strange at first, and most kids are super squeamish about you sticking a finger full of oil up their nostrils but lubricating the nose can be as important as cleaning it out. You can put it in with a little dropper or an option is to have the child do it himself. You could use most of the oils listed on Page 41 for massage, as well as ghee (see Page 43). Sometimes nose oil is mixed with Ayurvedic herbs or essential oils, but a little sesame oil goes a long way.

Say "aaahhh!"

Ayurveda looks at the tongue for clues on myriad issues. The tongue mirrors all of the organs and tells us what is going on in the digestive system. An Ayurvedic specialist can look at your child's tongue and have a very good idea of imbalances, including emotional imbalances and nutritional deficiencies. He can also gain much insight in observing the colour of the tongue, cracks, textures, and colour and quality of the tongue's coating.

Bad breath and a thick coating on the tongue (which in a healthy person would be pink with a slight white film) are signs that something is gunked up in the digestive system and a cold could be on the horizon. Parents can get good at this too, and a quick check of your child's tongue can be one more place to clue into her health.

Ayurveda suggests scraping your tongue in the morning as part of your daily oral health routine. You can buy a tongue scraper online and, in the meantime, use the edge of a spoon.

What did you say?

I've dealt with one ear infection in my seven plus years of being a mom of two. Firstly, my children were breastfed for many years, and that most certainly is a reason for the low infection rate. Also, at the slightest feeling of "soreness" in a child's ear, we're quick to put some warm oil in it (you can warm the bottle under the faucet or in a bain-marie style, by putting it into a cup of very hot water to warm). There are special blends made for children which include garlic oil, easily available in a health food store or online, though you could make these yourself. It's also a good idea to get in the habit of oiling their ears preventatively, just a little drop or two of sesame oil every couple of weeks.

ABHYANGA/SHANTALA MASSAGE

Massage. What do you think of when you think of massage? I hardly ever allowed myself the "luxury" of massage until I became pregnant, and then it was somehow like I finally deserved a massage. It was after having both kids and learning how to take care of myself again (assuming I was ever doing it in the first place) that I now give myself permission to see an Ayurvedic massage therapist at least every season. I used to think, *how dare I make time for myself in this way? How dare I not?* is the question. Ayurveda sees oil massage as crucial to optimal health. Obviously not only for adults, but children and babies too.

In India (and Europe and North America thanks to French obstetrician Frédérick Leboyer, who brought the technique here), parents massage their babies with oil as early as a month old, daily. This massage, called Shantala, is beneficial for countless reasons. Oil massage helps babies with gas, digestion and promotes a good sleep. It's also great for the immune system and seen as essential to the proper functioning of the lymphatic system and prana (vital energy).

Aside from nursing, massage is the next best way to bond with your child (the all-important skin to skin contact), so it's the perfect thing for fathers and mothers who do not breastfeed, to learn to do. There are courses a parent can take to learn this technique, although it is quite intuitive. I run regular workshops in Montreal and often the parents who come, leave feeling with a sense that they've been doing it "right" all along. You want to avoid massaging a fevered baby, and when massaging the belly always move clockwise.

What kind of oil to use?

The most important thing to think about is that our skin is our biggest organ and it absorbs everything we put onto it. There are many lotions and even baby massage oils that are filled with things we would not want moving through our blood stream. Stay away from mineral oil, which will block the pores (and is made from petroleum). The rule I use is, if I wouldn't drink it, I wouldn't put it on my skin, and especially not on my baby's skin. Good oils you have in your kitchen are the best. Ideally, they are raw and organic.

Different oils are best for different constitutions—for example, coconut oil is cooling (great for Pitta) while mustard oil is warming (good for Kapha). Sesame oil is helpful for grounding Vata babies and children and is tri-doshic, beneficial for each dosha. It's what I tend to recommend in my Shantala workshops.

Abhyanga is an oil massage that you could have a therapist do for you (this is one of my favourite things on the planet). He'll oil you up from head to toe—lots of warm oil on the head, and like Shantala, the therapist's strokes are rhythmic and move all the lymph around, stimulating the lymphatic and immune systems. Depending on your prakriti and the season, and what you need on that visit, he will adjust the technique and type of oil you need. Essential oils might also be added.

While it's worth seeing a pro (and there are other delicious types of Ayurvedic massage you would need to see one for) one of the beautiful things about Abhyanga is you can DIY (do it yourself) whether you're an adult or a child. It's recommended that you receive a daily massage and it can be done very quickly before the bath or in lieu of one. I repeat, *before* the bath to protect the skin from dryness. At the bare minimum, you could do a little massage with oil on your child's feet. As well as your own, of course.

Ayurveda also gets into the "subtle healing modalities" of Aroma, Sound, Colour, and Gem Therapy. These can be the most fun to use with kids because they appeal to the senses. See the resources and recommended reading section (Page 51) if this sounds interesting.

IN A YOGI MAMA'S PANTRY

Herbalism is a large part of Ayurveda. There are many simple and effective herbs and spices you can use to help prevent and cure illnesses if they manifest. The intricacies of the bio-spiritual model of herbalism are out of the scope of this book, but you do not need to be a herbalist or Ayurvedic specialist to effectively use plants and medicinal foods to support the health of your child and family.

Some of the more exotic-seeming Ayurvedic herbs like *Ashwagandha* and *Asafoetida* can be found in a health food store, herbalist shop or online, but here are some of the simplest, most useful herbs and spices I always have on hand, that you can get at the grocery store and likely already have in your kitchen.

Chamomile

Chamomile is a herb particularly good for your Pitta Child. It's a tea many people have in their homes and is safe for all ages (but related to ragweed, so take special care if there is suspicion of this allergy). It is calming, harmonizing and balancing. It helps with digestion and congestion; two things kids often need a little help with. It can be used as a poultice. This was one thing we used for the clogged tear duct my daughter had for the first months of her life. You can use the tea bag, cooled, to place on a wound. *Chamomilla* is the homeopathic chamomile remedy that many parents swear by for teething (myself included). Many herbalists would recommend not using this herb (unless in the homeopathic form) until allergies are ruled out, likely somewhere around six months. Many cultures, however, serve chamomile tea from a young age.

Note that in excess, chamomile increases Vata and can cause vomiting. So, like many things, it's best in moderation. The emetic quality can be counteracted if you add ginger (and ginger-chamomile tea is delicious for all ages).

Cinnamon

Cinnamon is heating and stimulating, and great for your Windy Kid. It decreases Vata and Kapha and increases Pitta, strengthening digestion. This spice helps with sinus issues, colds and congestion.

Raw honey

Fresh, raw honey is sattvic. It is warming and balances all of the doshas (though it can be a little aggravating for Pitta). It is nutritious and laxative and good to heal burns and wounds. We use it to soothe sore throats and just for a little treat because it is so healthy. It should never be heated. Bee propolis and pollen also have incredible healing properties.

Garlic

Is disinfectant, antiviral and antibacterial. It is also heating and rajasic, and for this reason not the best for your Fire Child to eat. Not that many children like eating garlic anyway. Because of its rajasic properties, it's generally avoided or minimized in Ayurvedic cooking, used more for medicinal purposes. You can use it to make ear oil to treat earaches or infections.

Ghee

Ghee, or clarified butter, plays a big role in Ayurveda. It's made by heating butter—preferably organic—and burning off all the water and milk solids. What you have is nutty, caramelly gold—a healthy fat with many benefits. It's sweet, cooling, tonic, rejuvenative and nutritious. It can help inflammation and improve digestion. Good, organic ghee is expensive, but making it is really easy and cost effective. It's something I do on a regular basis with my children. They love making it and they love eating it on everything. It has a high smoke point so it's the perfect choice for homemade popcorn, and it doesn't need to be refrigerated, so it spreads smoothly onto toast or bread.

You can use it in home remedies as a carrier for herbs or spices, and kids will be more than happy to just eat a big spoon of the sweet, nutty ghee (really, it doesn't taste anything like butter). As much as my kids recognize it as food, they are unfortunately a little reluctant to rub it onto their skin. They watch me use it in my nose, ears and even eyes (cooling for this Pitta Mama's tired eyes and can help with dark circles), and admittedly look a little horrified, but I know they'll come around.

Ginger

Ginger is an amazing remedy for colds and coughs. It is drying, and especially helps with wet coughs. I mix a tiny bit of ginger powder with raw honey and that is our "cough syrup." You can also use ghee instead of honey.

I also like to steep half a teaspoon each of ginger and cinnamon in a cup of hot water for about 10 minutes. This is a treat they look forward to if they happen to get sick. Ginger is an analgesic and relieves gas and cramps.

Onions

Okay, onions aren't a herb. But they are incredibly medicinal and always in my kitchen. They're the base for many Indian dishes, but they are tamasic and mostly discouraged as a food in Ayurvedic cooking.

A steamed onion poultice with a hot water bottle on the chest can work wonders to get rid of a deep-seated cough. I have also had much success with just putting a container of chopped raw onions beside my child's head at night, or in their socks. This trick isn't necessarily Ayurvedic, but it sure is useful.

Sesame oil

Sesame is the most nourishing of the vegetable oils. It is a wonderful oil for your Vata Child, as it calms nerves, anxiety and constipation. As mentioned previously, it's perfect for Abhyanga and for putting in the child's ears and nose. It also helps a dry cough.

Turmeric

Turmeric has definitely become a health fad in recent years—with good reason. People are cluing into its amazing health properties. It is good for the respiratory, digestive and circulatory systems. It can be used internally and externally. My favourite way to get turmeric into my kids' systems is with the delicious golden milk. There are many ways to make this healthy turmeric tea. I warm up nut milk blended with turmeric, cinnamon, ginger and dates. It's the perfect thing to put in your Vata Child's thermos in the winter. You can make it even more heating with black pepper and cayenne (which in my experience makes more of an adult version.)

YOGA AND YOUR CHILD

We can say that generally speaking, having an asana (yoga posture) practice is a great idea for everyone… but it depends on what that means to you. A person's prakriti should be taken into account when they're deciding when, where and how to "do yoga." If we go back to the example of that Fiery Mama who was aggravated by too much fire, it's likely that doing a 90-minute hot yoga class at noon (Pitta time) in the middle of July is not a good idea. Could a Vata person benefit from hot yoga in the winter? Probably.

While no one is taking their child to a hot yoga class (definitely not advised), it's just an obvious example of how our physical activities can be tailored to best suit our constitutions. A Kapha person would benefit less from a Yin Yoga practice (asanas held, on the ground, for 3-10 minutes) than a Pitta person, who needs that cool, dark, calm to contrast and balance their hot, active energy. Below are a few simple yoga postures and breathing techniques suggested for each dosha that you can practice with your children. Aside from yoga, you might consider activities like basketball or soccer for your Earth Child, who will benefit from invigorating sports, nourishing your Windy Kid's flexibility and energy with gymnastics, and putting your Fire Child in swimming or a team sport like hockey, to help her direct her desire to compete, in a healthy way.

Asana and pranayama for your Vata Child

So she is not "away with the wind," a Vata Child needs help becoming more grounded. Standing postures are excellent for this.

Vrksasana (Tree Pose)

Ask any child to strike a yoga pose and this will be the one he chooses. And it will be the wobbliest tree you've ever seen. This pose is about more than getting one foot on the thigh. Instruct your child to take a few comfortable breaths in *Tadasana* (Mountain pose, standing straight, feet under hips, palms facing out) weight balanced on both of the feet. Then, have him shift his weight to one foot. Keeping focused on an unmoving point, he can start to bring the other foot onto his leg—somewhere other than his knee. The whole point of the pose is to stay balanced, so if that means the toes stay on the ground like a little kickstand, there's no problem. It's perfect. Take a few breaths here and do the same on the other side. (See image of Millie on Page 13.)

Virabhadrasana I (Warrior 1)

Kids love to play in Warrior poses and there are many ways you can turn them into a game. For Warrior 1, have the child, from Mountain, step back with the left foot. Bend the right knee over the right ankle. Arms come above the head, vertical. The hips will naturally turn toward the front. There is enough width between the feet to allow for good balance, and between the arms so that it's comfortable between the shoulder blades. Breathe here and repeat on the other side.

Virabhadrasana II (Warrior 2)

Come into the pose from Mountain, left foot stepping back. Right knee is bent over right ankle. Back foot is strongly rooting down. Hips turn open and arms are horizontal. Have the child look out past the right fingertips. Your child can stay static in this pose or rock a little from back to front, imagining his yoga mat is a surfboard. Repeat on the other side.

Balasana (Child's Pose)

See instructions on page 48.

Calming Breath

Have your child sit with her knees bent and feet flat on the floor. If she's comfortable she can close her eyes. Then guide her to let her "out breath" (exhale) be a little longer than her inhale. You could even count for her, in for three and out for four or five seconds, following a count that is most natural for her.

Asana and pranayama for your Pitta Child

Seated forward folds, in general, bring the awareness inside and soothe the nervous system.

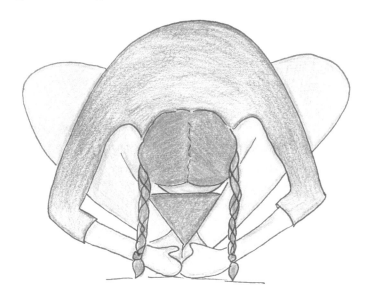

Baddha Konasana (Butterfly Pose)

Seated with soles of the feet "kissing each other" your child can round her spine into a forward fold. This is a cooling, Yin variation of the pose, and is even better if she can relax her forehead onto something like a pillow or block, or maybe her fists. Let her know that how "far" her head reaches is not important.

Paschimottanasana (Seated Forward Bend)

Start in *Dandasana* (Staff pose) sitting with legs outstretched in front. It could be a good idea to sit on a block or folded blanket. Like Butterfly, I propose to do this with kids as a gentle, Yin version and tell your child to be really careful with her neck.

Balasana **(Child's Pose)**

Have the child, with bent knees, sit back onto her feet. Fold the body forward over the thighs. Knees can be separated if it's more comfortable, and there are many different options for arm placement—however is most comfortable. (See image of Jayme on Page 17.)

Sitali Pranayama **(Cooling Breath)**

To help "cool down" a Fiery Child, cooling breath, like you see Jayme do on Page 17, can be very beneficial. Have your child curl her tongue, stick her tongue outside of her lips and inhale. She will immediately feel her mouth cool down, and the rest will follow suit. Some people can't roll their tongue, in which case, you could show your child to just sip air in as though she is sucking through a straw.

Chandra Bhedana **(Moon Breath)** can also be good for cooling and calming. Have the child sit comfortably and take a few normal, natural breaths, hands on thighs. When he's ready, he can bring his right hand toward his face. He'll close his right nostril with his thumb and inhale through the left nostril. On the exhale, he'll close his left nostril with his index finger and let the air come through the right side. Repeat, always inhaling through the left and exhaling through the right.

Asana and pranayama for your Kapha Child

Bhujangasana **(Cobra Pose)**

Cobra pose is a favourite for many kids. It is stimulating and invigorating and great for Earth Children. You can instruct your child to start on the belly. Bring the hands beside the ribs. Start to drag the mat towards your feet, like you're gliding up to lift the chest. The neck can stay long, and the child can come up just high enough so that it feels good for the lower back.

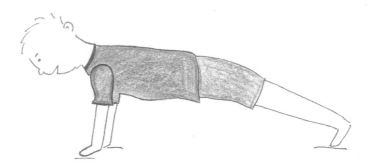

Phalakasana (Plank Pose)

Plank is fun and challenging. You can have the child start on hands and knees, supporting himself well with both hands. Walk the knees back and lift them. The body should come into a long, straight line (no cheating with the bum in the air!) While I really don't think it's a good idea to turn yoga into a competition, Plank challenges can be really fun for parents and children to do together. There's a good chance the parent will lose.

Virabhadrasana I, II (Warrior 1, 2)

(See instructions in the Vata Section, Page 45)

***Surya Namaskar* (Sun Salutations)** are also a great idea to stoke the fire and get the heart rate up. There are many variations. For children I like to teach it like this…

Mountain pose

Inhale: Arms over head for a slight backbend

Exhale: Fold forward, touch the ground by bending your knees as much as you need to

Walk or jump into plank

Come all the way to the belly

Cobra pose

Downward Facing Dog, like an inverted V

Walk or jump to the top of the mat for another forward fold

Inhale: Arms up and overhead, again for a slight back bend.

And repeat!

Surya Bhedana (Sun Breath)

It is energizing to inhale only through the right nostril. This breath will serve as a little pick me up when it's needed. Guide your child in the reverse of the above instructions for Chandra Bhedana (Page 48), inhaling through the right and exhaling left.

Resources and recommended reading

Fly Like a Butterfly by Shakta Kaur Khalsa

The Yoga Way to Radiance by Shakta Kaur Khalsa

Perfect Health for Kids: Ten Ayurvedic Health Secrets Every Parent Must Know by Dr. John Douillard

The Complete Book of Ayurvedic Home Remedies by Dr. Vasant Lad

Shantala: Un art traditionnel: le massage enfants by Frédérick Leboyer

The Yoga of Herbs: An Ayurvedic Guide to Herbal Medicine by Dr. David Frawley and Dr. Vasant Lad

Ayurveda and the Mind: The Healing of Consciousness by Dr. David Frawley